See how plants grow
Cereals

Nicola Edwards

WAYLAND

First published in 2007 by Wayland

Copyright © Wayland 2007

Wayland
338 Euston Road
London NW1 3BH

Wayland Australia
Hachette Children's Books
Level 17/207 Kent Street
Sydney, NSW 2000

British Library Cataloguing in Publication Data

Edwards, Nicola
   Cereals. - (See how plants grow)
   1. Grain - Juvenile literature
   I. Title
   584.9

   ISBN-13 978-0-7502-5004-7

Editor: Dereen Taylor
Designer: Elaine Wilkinson

Printed in China

Wayland is a division of
Hachette Children's Books.

The publishers would like to thank the following for allowing us to reproduce their pictures in this book:

Alamy: 4 (Dinodia Images), 7 (David Lyons), 20 (Carol & Mike Werner/Phototake Inc), 22 (Dave King/dk), 23 (Nigel Cattlin/Holt Studios). Corbis: cover and 17 (First/zefa), title page and 13 (Michael S. Yamashita), 9 (Adam Woolfitt), 10 (photocuisine), 12, 16, 19 (Terry W. Eggers), 21 (Owaki-Kulla). Ecoscene: 6 (Martin Jones). FLPA: 14 (Nigel Cattlin), 18 (Holt Studios). Panos: 5 (Mark Henley), 8 (Jeremy Hartley). Still Pictures: 11 (Jim Holmes), 15 (Joerg Boethling).

Contents

What are cereals?

Cereals are a group of plants that includes maize, rice and wheat. Cereal plants produce **seeds** called grains that we eat. Cereals are made into many different foods, such as bread, pasta and noodles.

▼ In India, grains of rice are the first food a bride gives to her husband.

▼ People all
over the world
eat more cereals
than any other
kind of food.

Where do cereals grow?

People have grown cereals for food for thousands of years. Cereal plants can grow on small patches of land or in big fields. Many people across the world depend on cereals for food.

▼ Rice is an unusual cereal plant because it grows under water.

Plants such as wheat and rice are often
grown on large farms. Some families in
Africa grow cereal plants such as millet,
sorghum or corn outside their homes.

This field of
corn belongs to a
family in Nigeria.

Cereals around the world

Cereal plants are found in most parts of the world. They cannot grow in deserts which are too dry or at the North and South Poles where it is too cold.

▼ This farmer is growing sorghum in Mauritania, north-west Africa.

Different cereals grow best in different **climates**. For example, sorghum and millet grow in hot countries while wheat prefers cooler temperatures.

▲ Oats are grown in areas that have a cool, damp climate, like Scotland.

What's in a grain?

A cereal grain is made up of different layers. A layer of **bran** covers the centre of the grain. The bran is rich in **fibre** and **vitamins** which we need for good health. The centre of the grain is high in energy-giving **starch**.

▲ As each grain is full of **nutrients** for the new plant, it's good for us to eat too.

Cereal Fact

In China, people greet each other by saying: 'Have you had your rice today?'

Within this starchy centre is the germ. The germ is the part of the grain from which new cereal plants grow.

The outer coatings of rice grain are being used as a **fertilizer**.

Planting seeds

Cereal plants are grown for food. Farmers prepare the ground to make sure the plants can grow well. They **plough** the fields where the seeds are to be sown. Paddy fields where rice is grown under water are flooded before planting.

This corn seed is germinating. Its **root** and shoot are beginning to grow.

Cereal Fact

Some countries plant cereal seeds by dropping them over large areas of fields from a plane.

Cereal seeds can be planted by hand or by machine. Seeds need to take in water before they can **germinate**, or start to grow.

The rice seedlings in this paddy field are being planted by hand.

The growing plant

When a cereal plant starts to grow, roots grow down from the seed and spread through the soil. The roots take in water and nutrients from the soil for the growing plant. Most cereal plants are grasses, with long, thin leaves.

▲ Cereal leaves have a sheath wrapped around the stem and a thin, veined blade.

Cereal Fact

Grasses grow in an unusual way. When grass is cut from the top it keeps on growing from underneath.

The leaves or blades of grass use sunlight, water and air to make food for the growing plant.

Can you see the roots on these rice plants?

Flowers and seeds

As cereal plants such as wheat and rice grow, they develop **heads**. These heads contain the **flowers** of the plant. The flowers have male and female parts.

▼ This field of barley is in flower.

The male part of the flower produces **pollen**. When the pollen enters the female part, new seeds begin to develop.

These heads of wheat have flowers inside them.

Harvesting cereals

Cereal plants change colour from green to gold as their seeds **ripen**. When the seeds are ripe they are ready to be gathered in or **harvested**. Farmers harvest cereals by hand or by using powerful machines.

These workers in Thailand are beating the bundles of rice so that the seeds will fall into the basket.

After harvesting, farmers separate the grains from the rest of the plant. The grains have to be completely dry before they are stored. Otherwise they may rot.

▲ This farmer in the USA is using a machine called a combine harvester to harvest the crop of wheat.

How do we use cereals?

People eat cereal grains, for example as cooked rice or barley, or in porridge made from oats or sorgum. We also grind wheat and maize grains into flour.

▼ How many foods can you think of that come from cereal plants?

The outer layers of rice grains can be burned as a fuel or turned into a fibre to make clothing.

▲ Cereal grains are used to feed farm animals such as cows, pigs and chickens.

Grow your own cereals

Plant some cereals such as wheat or corn and watch the plants develop. Soak the seeds in water overnight. Fill a container with soil. Gently push a few seeds into the soil until they are well covered.

▲ You could try planting different cereal seeds to compare how each type grows.

Cereal Fact

Rye is an unusual cereal plant because it can grow in poor soil on high land.

Water the soil to keep it damp.
When do the leaves appear?
What do they look like?

This wheat seed has germinated. A shoot is growing up from the seed while roots are spreading through the soil.

Glossary

bran
The outer layer of a cereal grain that is high in fibre.

climate
The patterns and types of weather that happen in different parts of the world.

fertilizer
A substance added to soil to help plants grow.

fibre
A substance found in plants that we eat to keep ourselves healthy.

flowers
The parts of a plant that produce pollen and from which fruits develop.

germinate
When a seed starts to develop into a new plant.

harvested
When a ripe crop is gathered from the place where it has been growing.

heads
The parts of a cereal plant that contain its flowers and in which seeds develop.

nutrients
Food in the soil that plants take in for growth.

plough
To prepare soil before seeds are planted in it.

pollen
The dust-like yellow substance produced by the male parts of plants and received by the female parts.

ripen
When a plant or a fruit becomes ready to be harvested or eaten.

roots
The parts of plants that anchor them in the soil and take in water and nutrients for growth.

seeds
The parts of a plant from which new plants develop.

starch
A substance found in some foods such as cereals that gives us energy.

vitamins
Substances found in foods such as cereals that we need to keep us healthy.

Index